Beauty Feng Shui

Chinese Techniques for Unveiling Your Inner Beauty

CHAO-HSIU CHEN

DESTINY

BOOKS

Destiny Books
Rochester, Vermont

P9-DDG-005

Destiny Books
One Park Street
Rochester, Vermont 05767
www.InnerTraditions.com

Destiny Books is a division of Inner Traditions International

Library of Congress Cataloging-in-Publication Data

Chen, Chao-Hsiu.
    [Feng shui fur schonheit und wohlbehinden. English]
    Beauty feng shui : Chinese techniques for unveiling your inner beauty /
Chao-Hsiu Chen.
       p. cm.
    ISBN 0-89281-852-2 (alk. paper)
    1. Beauty, Personal. 2. Feng-shui. I. Title: Chinese techniques for unveiling your
inner beauty. II. Title.

    RA778 .C422 2001
    646.7'26—dc21   00-047551

Printed and bound in the United States

10 9 8 7 6 5 4 3 2 1

Text design and layout by Priscilla Baker
This book was typeset in Garamond with Present as the display font

Beauty
Feng Shui

Contents

Beauty Changes the World

Many events in history have proven the ancient Chinese proverb, "No one crosses the gate of beauty without being damaged." In the history of the Empire of the Middle Kingdom, for example, there were three women whose beauty had a big impact on the political situation of the country—an impact that sometimes had negative consequences for the rulers. One of these beautiful women was the famous Shi-she, who lived around 500 B.C.E. She was born in the Yue Empire, which was at war with the Wu Empire. Since she was of supernatural beauty, a clever plan was conceived to marry her to the ruler of the Wu Empire in order to obtain his secret military plans. So it happened, and the Wu Empire was defeated.

The second woman who affected an empire was Chao-guen, who lived in the western Han dynasty. She was married to the ruler of Mongolia. The hope was that her beauty would entice him enough that he would forgo any future wars with the Han dynasty. This plan also played out.

A third case is that of Yang Yuhang from the Tang dynasty. Here is an example of how beauty can transform an entire culture. The time in which she lived is now commonly regarded in Chinese history as having produced the most significant works of art and literature. This is no wonder when one considers that the artists of this period were inspired by Yang Yuhang's beauty. Without her, the "golden age," as the Tang dynasty is often referred to, might never have happened.

Yet not only in China, but also in the Western world, there were women whose beauty changed the path of history: Cleopatra, Madame Pompadour, Lola Montez, Mata Hari, Wallis Simpson . . .

Beauty is the best that nature endows us with—this belief has held true for the past five hundred years. While today that viewpoint is still valid, health has been added to the equation, so that the two are now inextricably linked to one another. Most people want to be beautiful as well as healthy in order to feel good about themselves, to be loved, and to be successful. But they know that natural endowments are often not sufficient and that to attain this goal, one has to make certain efforts. The Chinese say: "Thirty percent natural endowment, seventy percent hard work." But what does "hard work" entail? It is certainly not the overwhelming use of makeup, but rather the art of making the best out of every one of nature's gifts. So how do you do that—especially when people are so different from one another?

There are many ways to attain this goal: the right clothing, proper makeup, diet, athletics, yoga, qi gong, and meditation, among others. Each of these methods has a certain result: more pronounced muscles, smoother movements, or a slimmer body. But none of these methods devised to enhance beauty deals with the whole body; instead, they all focus on either the internal or the external part of it. Moreover, they are often impractical and take up a lot of time or money.

Some people also think that they need plastic surgery in order to attain the look they desire. To this the Chinese say: "The external appearance is only a mirror image of the internal posture."

Can plastic surgery improve what is inside you? Certainly not—that is why you should work on your spirit and feelings in order to reach, along with the external appearance, a harmonious whole. And that is exactly what this book seeks to convey: how you, without substantial outlays of time or money, can attain the beauty results you want. The exercises that are presented here affect both internal and external parts and should become a part of your daily routine. That is how you can make the most out of your natural endowments, slow the process of aging, and perhaps even change the world . . .

In ancient China the body was viewed as a microcosm, or one small model of the larger universe. We are made up of yin and yang—the two complementary parts of the whole—female and male, light and dark. All living things also contain the five elements: wood, fire, earth, metal, and water. Each element corresponds to an internal organ: wood is related to the liver, fire rules the heart, the earth corresponds to the spleen, metal relates to the lungs, and water relates to the kidneys. In addition, we require wind, or air, to keep our bodies working.

Each of our individual bodies is linked to the larger universe, or macrocosm. The way menstrual cycles are affected by the moon is one example of how interconnected we are to the world at large. While it is difficult to change the macrocosm, the Chinese have developed numerous methods that are effective in dealing with the microcosm—our individual bodies. These methods include acupuncture, acupressure, natural medicine, and, of course, Feng Shui.

This five-thousand-year-old teaching comes from the observation of the natural world and its life cycles. It incorporates physical and psychological qualities in order to make health, happiness, and success permanent states of being. It was the Taoist priests who initially formed a teaching out of these observations. Feng Shui was refined over the course of time so that today we speak specifically of living, name, body, or beauty Feng Shui.

This book seeks to provide deep insight into the connection between humans and nature and into the unity of internal and external beauty. When you dive into this ancient Feng Shui secret, which incorporates the elements of qi gong, acupressure, and yoga, you will discover that you can suddenly have all that you have ever longed for . . .

Figure 1. Mei: Beauty

Figure 2. Tiao: Harmony

The Path to External Beauty

If you had to choose between a person whose face was beautiful but whose body was entirely out of proportion and one who had a well-proportioned body but an ugly face—which one would you choose? Most of us would prefer something in between—neither too ugly nor too beautiful. This statement expresses our desire for harmony, for proportionality, for a balance—something that applies not only to the body but also to the separate parts themselves. We will begin our journey to harmony with what we notice first: the face.

The Face:

THE COUNTENANCE OF A PURE PEACH BLOSSOM

The Chinese regard the face not only as the most important part of the human body, but also as the most important part of life at large. In China one's outward appearance is of such importance that it even recurs at the level of language: "to damage one's reputation" is described as "losing one's face." By now, of course, *loss of face* is an international term, which is why everyone tries to "save face."

Why do we consider one face beautiful and another ugly? It is certainly not just the natural endowments that we appreciate or disdain, but rather the sum of many details that attracts or repels us. Among these details are:

- the smile: friendly, false, sweet, charming, or fake

- the expression: worried, malicious, cool, unfriendly, nervous, downtrodden, sad, warm, innocent, relaxed, secure, attractive, wise, understanding, or benevolent

- the skin: smooth, silken, shiny, tough, rough, pale, scarred, red, or wrinkled

At first glance these three factors do not seem to go together. Consider, however, the smile, which comes from the lips and influences the expression, so that the expression can be discerned from the mouth—and of course from the eyes. (Since the expression of the eyes can only be changed from the inside, we will not discuss it at this point.) However, the skin, like the smile, is something that can be influenced from the outside—therefore the smile, expression, and skin are all facial characteristics that can be improved through external influences.

EXERCISES FOR THE FACE

1. Saliva-Increasing Chewing (Do with Every Meal)

This type of chewing increases the amount of saliva in the mouth. This leads to better digestion and stimulates the spleen, which is involved in the formation and destruction of red blood cells. The circulation of the blood in turn influences the muscles and the condition of the skin.

Keep your mouth closed while chewing. Grind the food slowly

and disperse it evenly in your mouth. Move your upper and lower jaws strongly without opening your lips. Chew on both sides simultaneously. The movements should be felt all the way to the end of the cheekbones.

This exercise helps in strengthening the cheek muscles. This avoids wrinkles and makes the skin smooth, the smile more attractive, and the overall expression positive.

2. Oxygen-Stimulating Facial Cleansing (Apply with Every Washing of the Face)

This type of facial cleansing strengthens the consistency of the pores, which enables the skin to take in more oxygen and thus breathe better.

- Remove makeup from your face using a cotton ball dipped in makeup remover. Always rub from the top down, never upward, since that would bring dirt and makeup into the pores and clog them, which will cause skin impurities.

- Fill your hands with lukewarm water and slowly pull it into your nose by leaning forward and "inhaling" the water; blow it out with all your strength right away. Repeat this process until you see that the released water is entirely clean.

- Now wash your face as you usually do, but with cold water. Dry it.

- Use either dry hands or hands wet with water from your face to slap your forehead nine times using your right hand while at the same time slapping your chin nine times with your left hand.

- Now slap your right cheek nine times with your right hand while doing the same thing to your left cheek using your left hand. Repeat with crossed hands.

Keep your eyes closed while doing this and don't slap too softly, but rather hard enough that you feel a small amount of pain.

These exercises help strengthen the facial muscles and prevent skin impurities and wrinkles. Cleansing the nose with water keeps its mucous membranes smooth and helps in fighting off colds.

3. Acupressure Creams
(Apply after Each Washing)

Skin also needs the proper nutrition: The skin cells that die off during the day due to outside influences regenerate during the night. Therefore, it is important to use a protective cream for the daytime and an appropriate regeneration cream at night. In both cases there are many excellent skin and season-specific products. Nonetheless you should never overuse these products; the secret of beautiful skin is on the inside, not just the outside. It is thus better to use less and even better to use it properly.

Apply the cream to forehead, chin, and cheeks. Then place your elbows at your sides, lifting your arms up to your chest. Straighten out your spinal cord, breathe normally, and close your eyes. Using the fingertips of your right hand, rub the cream from your right temple to your left temple in eight circular motions. The ninth movement goes along your cheekbone to your chin. With your left hand, make the same movement in the other direction (diagram A).

Now treat the area above your lips by massaging the cream with your right hand from the right corner of your mouth to the left corner and back to the right in nine circular motions. Do the same thing in the reverse direction with your left hand (diagram B).

Use the insides of your hands to massage the remaining cream onto your cheeks in circular motions, until it has been fully absorbed.

Place both middle fingers at the root of the nose and press between your eyebrows and the closed eyes in a circular motion around the eyes. Diagram C shows the eight acupressure points. Repeat this exercise three times.

When you apply cream to your face in this manner you not only save a lot of time, but you will also soon notice that your skin has changed: it is now smoother, softer, and significantly less wrinkled.

Place both thumbs on the chi points behind your earlobes (the points where you would normally apply perfume) and move both hands nine times in the direction of your chin—not too slowly and not

too fast (diagram D). Close your eyes while doing this and open them again only after your ninth movement. Repeat this exercise three times.

E

Take a deep breath. Release your breath forcefully and, while doing this, rapidly pat down the area between your nose and chin (around the mouth) using your fingertips (diagram E). The tapping of your fingers should resemble the staccato of a piano piece. Repeat this exercise four times in a row.

If the above exercises are carried out correctly, they will lead to better circulation in the skin—and thus to a more beautiful appearance.

The Neck

SUPPLE STRENGTH OF BAMBOO IN THE WINDS OF LIFE

Most people focus on the face or body of others, but rarely direct their attention to the neck. In contrast, when looking at Asian, ancient Egyptian, Greek, or Roman sculptures, it is obvious that the sculptors of those time periods placed great emphasis on the neck. The current Western neglect of the neck is strange, especially when one considers that this region is a highly erogenous zone. Necklaces, scarves, and ties all highlight the importance and beauty of the neck. Thus we want to present some exercises so that—regardless of whether it is thin, thick, short, or long—the neck will be viewed as equally important to the other body parts, not lastly

Figure 3. Tao Hua: Peach Blossom

because it carries our head—for our entire lives. It is thanks to its strength that we not only have a field of vision of 270 degrees but can also speak, breathe, eat, smell, hear, and kiss.

EXERCISES FOR THE NECK

1. Water for the Pillar of Heaven
(Do in the Morning after Washing)

There are eight important meridian points on the neck. It is necessary to stimulate each through a slight beating in order to rejuvenate the circulation.

Take some water in your hands and apply it to your neck with small slaps, first slapping the front nine times using your right hand, and then the sides using both hands. Repeat this with your left hand and then with both hands. Repeat the entire process one more time, always keeping a straight posture.

2. Acupressure Exercise
(Do in the Morning after Washing)

Place both thumbs on the chi points behind the earlobes and move both hands toward the chin—moving neither too slowly nor too quickly. Close your eyes while doing this and open them only after completing the exercise. Repeat this process three times (you will also find this exercise among the exercises for the face; see step D on pages 11–12).

3. Chi Exercise
(Do in the Evening after Washing)

Stand up with your legs slightly spread and exhale for as long as possible while forming an F sound with your lips. Then inhale as

Figure 4. Gin Tzu: The Strength of Bamboo

deeply as possible while simultaneously leaning your neck backward and pulling up your shoulders. Hold your breath for as long as possible and then return to the starting position. Exhale as described above. Repeat this exercise three times.

In the beginning it is possible that you will experience neck pain. Don't worry; this is a normal reaction, as we rarely move that part of the neck. If you repeat this exercise frequently you will find that your neck-shoulder line will become stronger and more beautiful. Moreover, the third exercise leads to a sounder sleep, which also has a positive influence on beauty.

These exercises should also become a part of your daily routine; they take up hardly any time but are highly effective—especially if you continue to do them.

The Arms
HUNDREDFOLD BRANCHES REACHING TO THE SKY

The only way to exercise all the muscles of the body is through swimming, which has the additional advantage of bringing about balanced arm muscles. No workout in which biceps and triceps are under extreme stress can bring about results comparable to those of swimming—especially if the muscles are being exerted unevenly. The objective should not be to amass the biggest muscles, but rather to reach a balance that will be reflected in smooth body lines. The upper arm muscles are at the greatest risk of losing their consistency during aging. However, since not everyone can go swimming on a daily basis, three exercises are presented here that enhance balanced body lines as well as a better muscle consistency.

EXERCISES FOR THE ARMS

1. One-Third to Two-Thirds Walking
(Do whenever You Are Walking)

Stand up straight. Walk in such a way that the balls of your feet make contact first, followed by the heels. Move your arms so that your lower arms swing loosely one-third of the way in front of you, and then two-thirds of the way around to the back. Don't rely on doing this automatically, but make a conscious effort until this movement comes naturally to you. If you feel unobserved, you can even throw your arms backward until the backs of your hands lightly touch your buttocks. These movements activate your meridians, which improves the circulation of blood through your body.

2. Nine Points on the Wall
(Do whenever You Want to Overcome Fatigue)

Stand in front of a wall or a door. Make sure that your head, hands, buttocks, and heels touch the wall or door. Focus on a point that is slightly above your usual field of vision. Exhale as much as you can and then inhale deeply, while bringing your elbows up to shoulder level and standing on tiptoes. Hold your breath for as long as you can while keeping this position. Then exhale and allow your feet and hands to return to their usual position, while slightly bending your knees. Repeat this exercise four times in a row.

3. Five Breaths in X
(Do before Taking a Shower)

Stand with your legs slightly spread. Hold your arms up high while crossing your hands so that the palms rest on top of one another. Exhale all the way (diagram A). Now inhale slowly while at the

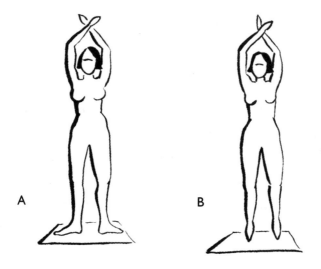

same time rising to your tiptoes. Hold your arms up even higher (diagram B). Exhale and bend your knees while remaining on your tiptoes (diagram C). Inhale again and stretch your legs (diagram D). Exhale and return your feet to their normal position. Now let your arms drop to your sides (diagram E).

Naturally, this exercise is also suitable for buttock, leg, and chest muscles. While it might seem a little complicated, it has many positive effects.

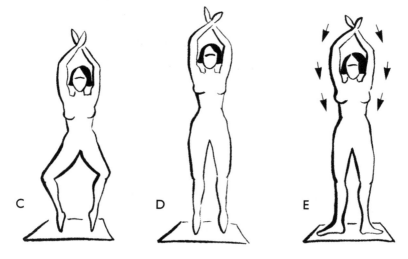

Figure 5. Wan Nan: Arms that Reach for the Sky

The Breasts

MOUNTAINS OF ETERNAL LIFE

What is it about the female breasts that makes them so attractive that hardly anyone is able to ignore them? Psychoanalysts believe our fascination stems from infancy—when breasts were a source of food and nurturance. The breasts are a symbol of femininity, though they unfortunately change shape with the passage of time. We must pay careful attention to maintaining their shape throughout the years. That is why *Beauty Feng Shui* contains exercises designed for all types of breasts, not just those depicted in men's magazines.

EXERCISES FOR THE BREASTS

1. Chest Breathing in X
(Do before or after Showering)

Repeat the exercise "Five Breaths in X" from the arm section (pages 17–18).

2. Acupressure Exercise
(Do while Showering)

With your right hand, reach for your left breast and glide with one strong but slow movement in the direction of your armpit, slowly bringing your thumb and middle finger together. Do the same with your right breast, using your left hand. Repeat this exercise nine times.

3. Acupressure Exercise
(Do in Bed before Going to Sleep)

Place both hands on your ribs below your breasts, with the two middle fingers touching. Forcefully exhale for nine seconds. While holding your breath, rub your hands over your breasts toward your neck in one strong stroke. Let your arms drop to your sides and take a slow and deep breath, so that your chest rises. Repeat this exercise eight times.

Exercises 2 and 3 are designed to increase the chest size of both men and women.

The Hips
WILLOW BRANCHES IN THE EMPIRE OF THE MIDDLE KINGDOM

Eroticism is never expressly described in Chinese literature; rather, images from other areas (especially nature) are used to convey the message. For example, a poem from the Tang dynasty about a prostitute from the Jangtse River says:

> *Her arms are tender,*
> *like the leaf patterns of the willow,*
> *whose branches her hips resemble.*

In the Empire of the Middle Kingdom, slender hips have always been a beauty ideal—which is also true for the Western world. Consider, for example, the widespread use of corsets during the French rococo period. Even today slender hips are in vogue, which is why many women feel the need to attain this shape through constant dieting. However, most diets prove disappointing, since it is impossible to directly affect specific parts of the body.

Figure 6. Fon Le: The Joy of the Top

EXERCISES FOR THE HIPS

1. Exercise
(Do before Going to Sleep in Bed or on the Floor)

Lie down and spread your arms as far apart as possible. Press your palms onto the bed or floor. Press your knees together and bring your legs upward. Concentrate on your hips, focusing your eyes on the ceiling and swinging your legs from left to right. Do not open your knees, but touch the mattress or floor with them while keeping your head straight.

2. Exercise
(Do while Sitting Up)

Prolonged sitting often causes the hips as well as legs to increase in width. The following exercise is designed to prevent this and to ease back, shoulder, and neck aches.

Buy three foam rubber cushions of various sizes and place them on a chair as shown in the illustration. Tie them to the chair so that they won't move. Sit down on the chair, keeping your back straight and pulling your stomach in. Keep your feet flat on the floor.

3. Exercise
(Do while Walking)

This exercise is almost identical to "One-Third to Two-Thirds Walking" exercise (see page 17). Keep yourself steady and upright and

Figure 7. Fon Liou: The Wind in the Meadows

walk so that the balls of your feet make contact with the ground first, followed by your heels. Move your arms as described in the walking exercise. Do not rely on having this happen automatically but focus on it until it happens naturally. Make sure that the strength comes from your hips and not from your thighs.

To better understand and complete this exercise, think about how you move forward when swimming on your back or freestyling: the "engine" is always in the hips, while the arms are the "wheels." In tennis or golf, too, the strength of the arm movement does not come from your arms, but from the hips. The slimmer your hips are, the better your movement will be.

The Abdomen
SMALL HILL, GOOD FORTUNE

It generally holds true that the female body stops changing for the better after reaching age thirty; for men the turning point comes when they reach fifty. The cause for this is our upright stance. The legs have to carry all the weight, while the joints get worn down over time. As the joints in the hip wear down, this leads to wider hips and thus most often to a bigger abdomen.

Further reasons for a protruding, thick, or flaccid stomachs are improper diets (too much fat), as well as improper ways of eating. If you eat too hastily, too much air will get into the stomach along with the food. The gases created lead to a swollen abdomen that can only be remedied through a comprehensive change in eating habits.

The following guidelines will help you maintain a well-shaped abdomen even in old age:

1. Eat a low-fat diet.
2. Chew your food thoroughly and then swallow slowly.
3. While eating, concentrate on your food. Do not read, watch TV, or do anything else.
4. Divide the quantities of your meal according to the following ratio. 3 (breakfast) : 2 (lunch) : 1 (dinner). Do not eat after 7 P.M. Drink only after, not during, your meals.
5. Sit upright as often as possible. Practice this according to the illustration on page 23.

As a result of proper eating, the expanded stomach will go back to its normal size, looking tight and trim.

EXERCISES FOR THE ABDOMEN

1. Exercise for the Release of Gas (Do before Going to Sleep)

Lie down on your back. Take a deep breath and use both hands to bring your right leg upward (diagram A). Exhale and bring the leg in to your chest (diagram B). Repeat steps A and B with your left leg.

A

B

Now exhale and bring both legs slightly upward with your hands (diagram C). Exhale and bring both legs to your chest (diagram D).

Repeat this exercise four times to allow gases to be released. This is nothing to be embarrassed about but rather is a part of healthy living.

2. Exercise for the Improvement of the Stomach Muscles (Do before Going to Sleep)

Lie down on your back, with your palms touching the bed or floor. Keep your legs together (diagram A). Exhale and slowly lift both

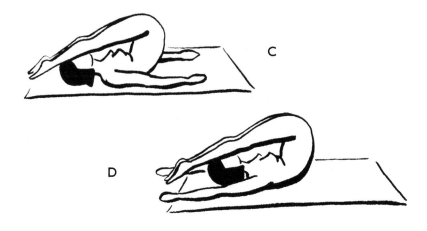

legs until they reach a 90 degree angle (diagram B). Extend both legs over your head until they touch the bed or floor (diagram C). Keep breathing normally. Reach behind your head with your hands and touch your toes (diagram D).

3. Exercise for the Strengthening of the Stomach Muscles (Do Whenever Possible)

Stand up straight and press your knees and feet closely together. Take a deep breath (diagram A). While exhaling, lean forward and try to

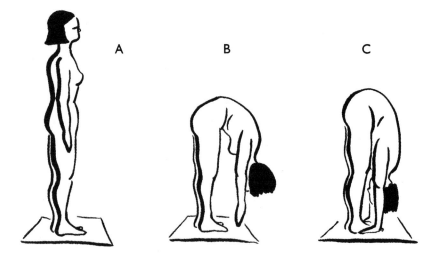

touch your toes (diagram B). Inhale deeply and, while exhaling, try to press your head against your calves (diagram C). Slowly "roll" back upward while concentrating on feeling each abdominal muscle.

All three of these exercises also have beneficial effects on the back and leg muscles, as well as improving the circulation of blood through the brain.

The Buttocks

GINKGO MAGIC AT THE BEGINNING OF THE END

Goethe was amazed by the leaf of the ginkgo tree, since it is impossible to say whether it consists of two parts, or one part that has separated. The same applies to the human buttocks, which consist of two halves, each a mirror image of the other. For both men and women this part of the body always seems to be a problem: it is never perfectly proportioned. But the buttocks are objects of interest to the opposite sex. To improve the tone and proportions of your buttocks, the following exercises are suggested.

EXERCISES FOR THE BUTTOCKS

1. Exercise
(Do before Showering)

Identical to the third arm exercise (pages 17–18).

2. Exercise
(Do before Going to Sleep)

Identical to the first hips exercise (page 23).

3. Exercise
(Do while Sitting)

Identical to the second hips exercise (page 23).

Figure 8. Shao Fu Da Fu: Small Hill, Good Fortune

4. Exercise
(Do before Going to Sleep)

Lie down on your right side (diagram A). Lift your left leg while inhaling deeply, keeping your toes pointed (diagram B). Exhale while bringing your leg forward to a 45 degree angle, then place it on the floor (diagram C). Inhale, lift the leg, and bring it to a 45 degree angle behind you. Keep it in the air for nine seconds (diagram D). Exhale and return the leg to its initial position (diagram A). Turn over onto your left side and repeat the exercise with your right leg.

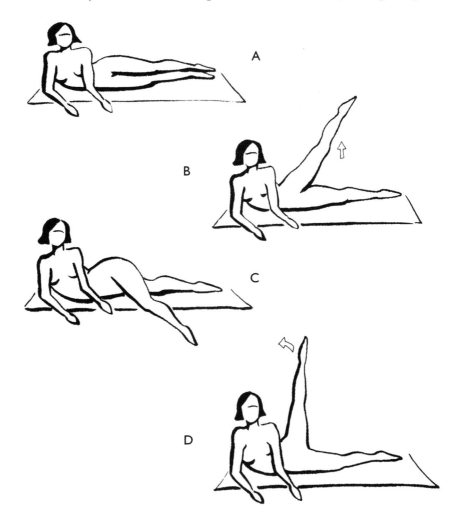

5. Exercise
(Do before Going to Sleep)

Lie down on your stomach, with your forehead touching the floor or bed. Press your palms against on the floor or your mattress at hip level, contracting your leg and buttock muscles and stretching through the toes (diagram A). Take a deep breath and lift your upper body (diagram B). Exhale and push your upper body back as much as possible (diagram C). This exercise is also good for relieving constipation and increasing your lung capacity.

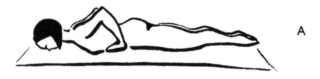

A

B

C

Figure 9. In Shin Yie: Ginkgo Leaf

The Legs

ROOTS IN MOTION

The custom of binding women's feet—popular in China for hundreds of years—was not beneficial for women, at least from today's vantage point. By the age of two or three, bound feet would already be irreparably damaged—to the extent that girls could never place them flat on the floor. This occurred because the wrapping of the feet began when the bones were still soft, in an effort to keep the feet from growing at all. Moreover, the bandages were rarely changed. The objective of this procedure was to increase the appeal of women: bandaged feet made the legs appear longer, and large feet were considered ugly. Since natural balance was no longer possible, women had to tiptoe instead of walk, which led to the breasts and buttocks sticking out more than usual. The modern counterpart to this practice is high heels, which are supposed to have the same effect—artificially elongating the calves. Not every woman can wear heels, but there are other ways of making the lines of the legs appear longer than normal if you so choose.

EXERCISES FOR THE LEGS

1. Exercise
  (Do before Showering)

This exercise is identical to the third exercise for the arms (pages 17–18).

2. Exercise
  (Do before Going to Sleep)

This exercise is identical to the fourth exercise for the buttocks (page 31).

3. Exercise
(Do before Going to Sleep and Shortly after Waking Up)

Lie on your back, keeping your legs together. Take a deep breath and stretch out your feet as forcefully as possible toward the foot of the bed (diagram A). Exhale and turn your feet outward while keeping your legs together (diagram B). Slightly lift your legs and, using your feet, draw a small circle in the air, from left to right. Draw nine circles while keeping your legs lifted (diagram C). Repeat this with circles from right to left (diagram D).

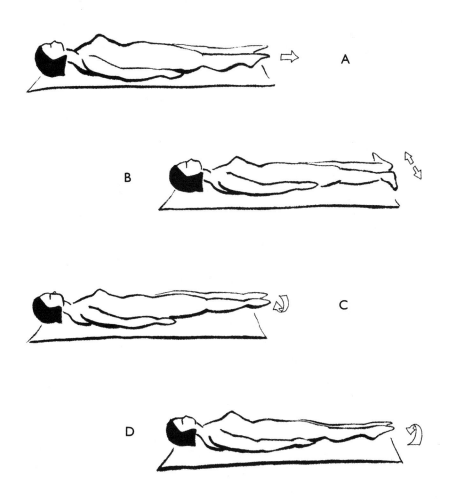

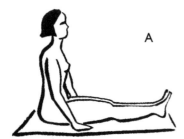

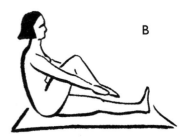

4. Exercise
(Do Anytime)

Sit down on the floor and stretch out your legs and feet (diagram A). Bring your right leg toward you and grab your heel with both hands (diagram B). Exhale and bring the leg all the way toward you, while slowly straightening it (diagram C). Repeat this with the other leg.

Figure 10. Gao Gen Shie: High Heels

The Skin

MORNING DEW AS SMOOTH AS JADE

The capacity for invention in today's cosmetics industry is immense. Almost every day a new product becomes available that is supposed to protect, nourish, embellish, and improve skin. Do you buy a product because you have been influenced by advertising or do you experiment with different ones before deciding on the best for you? We all know that truly beautiful skin is not attainable through outside influences alone. A healthy diet, physical condition, and emotional outlook are also necessary for positive results.

In order to have healthy skin, your body needs:

1. sufficient sleep
2. a balanced diet
3. regular hygiene
4. psychological stability
5. acupressure exercises

The following exercises, which come from traditional Chinese medicine, can be carried out at any time.

EXERCISES FOR THE SKIN

1. Exercise

Rub your hands together until they become hot. Lift your chin up as high as possible and rub slowly up and down the neck with the fingers of each hand (not with the thumbs), as shown in diagram A.

2. Exercise

Press on the acupressure points shown in diagram B with three fingers of each hand, moving from the top down, a total of thirty-six
times.

B

3. Exercise

With three fingers of each hand, press on the eye points shown in
diagram C. Exhale while pressing on the points; release them when
you inhale. Repeat this exercise nine times.

C

The Hair

WATERFALL OF SILK

Beautiful hair is much more than a beautiful hairstyle. It is shiny,
healthy hair that looks great no matter what. To keep your hair
looking its best, be sure to:

- find the right products for your hair type

- treat hair gently, whether it is wet or dry

- evaluate your lifestyle if you are experiencing excessive hair
  loss (not related to a medical problem)

- carry out the following exercises as frequently as possible

Figure 11. U Lu Zao Zuen: Morning Dew as Smooth as Jade

Figure 12. Sse Pu: Waterfall of Silk

EXERCISES FOR THE HAIR

1. Exercise

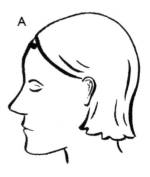

Rub your hands together until they are hot. While exhaling, tap your fingertips against the top of your forehead, at your hairline (diagram A). Inhale and repeat the tapping. Do this exercise four times.

2. Exercise

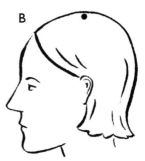

Again, rub your hands until they are warm. Exhale and tap your finger on the middle of the top of your head (diagram B). Do not tap while inhaling. Repeat this exercise four times.

3. Exercise

Rub your hands together until they are hot. Exhale and tap behind your ears, where your hair starts (diagram C). Do not tap while inhaling. Repeat this exercise four times.

Figure 13. Shian I: Fitting Together

Feminine Concerns

Buddhism states that all existence is suffering. Short spurts of happiness are followed by long stretches of sadness and worry. We are surrounded by problems, and the constant fear of failing health. Even the mere act of worrying about our health seems to contribute to physical and psychological ills. If we perceive ourselves as bad or ugly, we further compound these effects. This chapter addresses these concerns and offers exercises intended to restore and improve our quality of life.

Oily Face

If your skin is unable to hold makeup for long periods of time, the problem may be the quality of your skin. Glandular problems must be treated by a doctor, but the prescribed therapy can be supplemented by the following exercise.

Kneel down like a sprinter on a starting block (diagram A). Bring your head to the floor as if you were about to do a headstand. Stretch both legs backward so you resemble a mountain (diagram B). Bring the tips of your feet nine times to the front, nine times to the back, nine times right, and nine times left (diagram C).

Make sure that your head and hands do not move during this exercise, your chin is resting on your chest, and your eyes are focused on the floor.

A

B

C

Freckles

According to traditional Chinese medicine, this pigment irregularity is linked to a malfunctioning of the adrenal gland. This, of course, can only be treated by a doctor—even though it will not lead to a disappearance of the freckles. However, if you want to try to lighten some of your freckles, try the exercise below.

Lie down flat and then raise your back and legs to a 30 degree angle from one another. Press your hands against your chest in a defensive position. Slowly inhale (diagram A). Forcefully press your hands forward while exhaling with an F sound (diagram B). Bring your hands and legs back against your chest and inhale (diagram C). Repeat step B and lie down flat again (diagram D). Repeat this exercise four times a day.

A

B

C

D

Figure 14. Sai Shue: Whiter than Snow

Many skeptics will immediately doubt that gymnastics routines can affect the skin. While it may seem counterintuitive, the exercises put forth in *Beauty Feng Shui* are based on knowledge that has been gathered and passed on for millennia. The previous exercise, for example, is a form of yoga that stresses proper breathing technique. It is important to note that breathing affects our health just as much as physical exercises. Of course, results won't be noticeable right away, but rather will be apparent only after months or years of effort. However, these exercises, when done over time, will greatly improve your health. They do not have any negative side effects, they are simple and can be carried out anywhere, anytime, and they will make you feel good. Start today.

Acne

The main cause of this skin ailment is a disruption of the hormonal system. Additionally, bad diets, stress, and psychological problems can also lead to acne. The following exercise can bring your hormones back into balance.

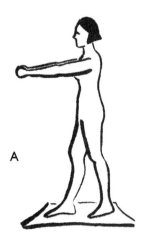

A

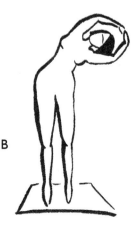

B

Stand with your legs spread and interlock the fingers of your outstretched hands (diagram A). Inhale and lift your hands over your head. While you exhale, move your upper body from right to left with your back slightly bent. Use the strength of your hips to do this. Inhale again and return to your starting position while exhaling (diagram B). Repeat this exercise eight times.

Rough Skin

There are many factors that can cause rough skin: sunburn, a bad diet, substance abuse, stress, and so forth. The following exercise helps skin breathe better and promotes quicker cell regeneration.

Lie flat on your back and pull your legs up slightly. Rub your hands until they are hot. Place your hands on your lower stomach. Exhale nine times while pressing on this spot (diagram A). Now form a bridge without the aid of your hands, making sure that your spinal cord is straight. Inhale while doing this (diagram B). Exhale and return to the starting position (diagram C).

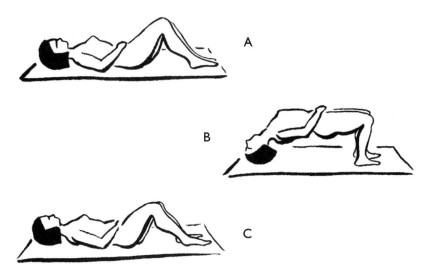

A

B

C

Figure 15. Shon U: More Beautiful than Jade

Figure 16. Xe Zou: Smooth as Silk

Repeat this exercise four times, always very slowly and consciously. Do not get up immediately after the exercise but rather lie down for another five minutes while breathing normally. While doing step B, it is important not to place your entire weight on your neck and head.

Puffy Face

The use of cortisone, the abuse of alcohol, and kidney ailments can each cause your face to swell. In these cases please see a doctor—the following exercise is not designed for ailment-induced cases, but rather those stemming from a lack of sleep or excessive exertion.

Lie on your right side, as shown in diagram A. Exhale and bring your left leg forward to a 90 degree angle (diagram B). Now turn your torso so that you can rest your face in your hands. Look straight ahead and stay in this position for ten seconds (diagram C). Next, lie on your left side and repeat this exercise. Repeat the entire process four times.

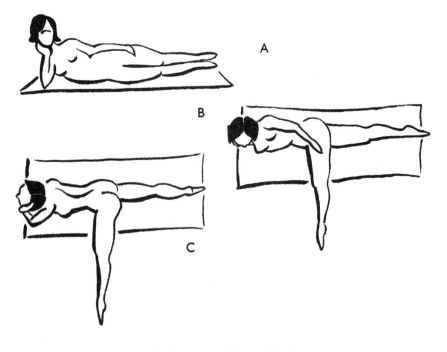

Double Chin

Double chins develop as people get older, when the skin loses its elasticity. Some people then look for a plastic surgeon, but there are yoga exercises that—if practiced early on—can make surgery unnecessary.

Sit on your knees. Relax and look straight ahead (diagram A). Look at the ground while pressing your chin to your collarbone. Exhale and slowly move your head to the left (diagram B). Inhale and slowly lift your head up and backward, as far as you can (diagram C). Exhale, straighten your head, and face forward (diagram D). Bring your chin back down to your collarbone and stop breathing for nine seconds. Inhale again and return to the starting position (diagram E).

Repeat this exercise in the other direction and do the whole process four times.

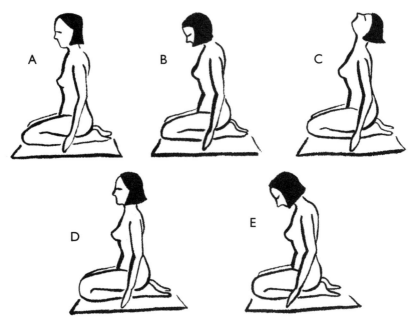

Menstrual Problems

Just before each monthly menstrual period, many women experience a collection of symptoms (water retention, headaches, abdominal cramps, low backache, irritability) commonly known as premenstrual syndrome (PMS). PMS comes from a hormonal imbalance that needs to be treated by a doctor. Here we will deal mainly with the abdominal cramps that occur during menstruation itself. The following exercise helps alleviate these pains.

Lie on your back, keeping your arms at your sides while pressing them against the mattress or floor. Take a deep breath (diagram A). Hold your breath and lift your legs to a 45 degree angle (diagram B). Exhale, then inhale. Now, using your feet, draw a clockwise circle in the air (diagram C).

Repeat the exercise, this time drawing a counterclockwise circle at step C. Repeat the entire process four times.

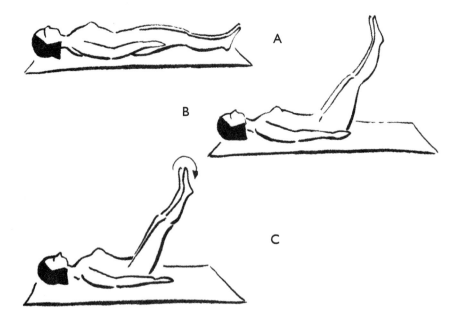

Figure 17. Hwei Fu: Recuperating

Figure 18. Gu: Stability

Menopausal Problems

The hormonal changes that occur during menopause can cause many physical and psychological problems. The following exercise should help alleviate these symptoms so that you can continue to feel young and attractive.

Lie flat on your back. Press your palms against the mattress or floor. Lift your left leg to a 90 degree angle while keeping it straight. Breathe normally (diagram A). Now lift your right leg to 30 degrees and change the position of the two legs in rapid succession, altogether thirty-six times. Don't mix up this exercise with the popular "cycling"; always remain in the 30 or 90 degree position. Use your abdominal muscles to swing your legs (diagram B).

A

B

Figure 19. Tiao Ho: Regulating

Figure 20. Hwei Zuen: The Return of Spring

Wrinkles around the Eyes

Unfortunately, age brings not only valued wisdom, modesty, and inner calm, but also the loss of hair, shrinking height due to the regression of intervertebral discs, and wrinkles, especially around the eyes, which also lose their shimmer. The first exercise is designed to gain back the shimmer, the second to prevent wrinkles.

1. Exercise

Relax while standing upright, with your feet slightly apart. Rub your hands until they are hot. Cover your left eye with your left hand. With your right eye, look up and down six times in a row, moving your eye as quickly as possible. Then move your right eye from left to right and back six times in a row, again moving it as quickly as possible. Then try twelve times to move your eye diagonally (from top right to bottom left, then in the reverse direction). Finally, let your eye roll six times (first from right to left, then from left to right). Again rub your hands until they are hot, then place your right hand on your right eye and repeat the exercise.

2. Exercise

Using your middle fingers, press against the acupressure points indicated in diagram A. Exhale completely while you do this. Remove your fingers from the acupressure points in an abrupt movement and inhale as deeply as possible. Repeat this exercise six times.

A

Then, using the same method, press on the points indicated in diagram B.

Repeat again with the points indicated in diagram C. Now rub your hands until they are hot and place them on your eyes for thirty seconds.

Constipation, Lack of Appetite, Cold Hands and Feet

At first glance these three symptoms do not seem to be related to one another. Nonetheless, Taoist medicine knows that there are three important meridian points in the body that can have a positive influence on all three symptoms. They can be activated as follows.

Kneel down so that your buttocks are touching the heels of your feet. Keep your back straight and contract your anus. Inhale, rub your hands until they are hot, and place them on the points indicated in diagram A (about three inches above the coccyx). While exhaling, rub these spots until they are hot.

Diagram B shows the meridian point situated at the intersection of the spine and waist. Stimulate this point in the same way you stimulated the two others.

Both exercises should be performed four times.

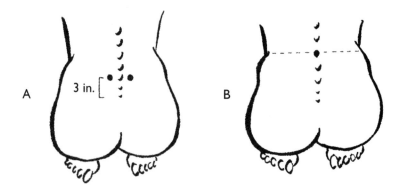

Figure 21. Min Lian: Shine

Figure 22. Shun Hwan: Circulation

Lumbago Pains, Flatulence, Swollen Feet

As we alluded to in the previous section, the secret of healing through acupressure is knowing the locale of those meridian points that can alleviate symptoms. The points are not necessarily in the same area as the symptoms, so don't be surprised when the following exercises show points that seem far removed from the part that hurts. To alleviate the three above-mentioned symptoms, you should do the following.

Stand with your legs together and rub your hands until they are hot. Inhale deeply, then massage the places indicated in diagram A while exhaling. Repeat this four times. Then repeat the exercise with the points shown in diagrams B and C.

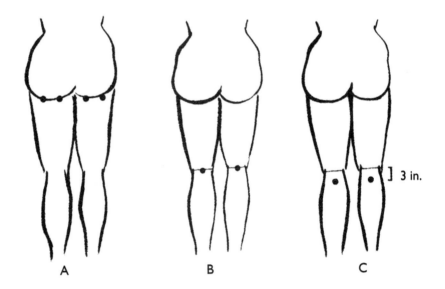

A   B   C

Figure 23. Chang: Strength

The Way to Inner Beauty

$\mathcal{I}$t has already been mentioned that the external appearance is merely a reflection of the internal condition. Thus, if you want to be beautiful on the outside, start working on your inner self as early as possible. Studying the interaction of the poetic and philosophical thoughts of different cultures is one way to accomplish this. Another is playing music or creating art; a third is a compassionate volunteer approach. However, all this still has to do with the outside, since a true recourse to oneself can be done only through internal contemplation. How this is accomplished and how it can contribute to beauty will be clarified in some detail in the following chapter.

Meditation

THE ART OF RETREATING INSIDE

To understand all the implications of meditation, one has to know that meditation is a highly complex activity. While Westerners may view meditation as sitting peacefully and resting, it is actually an advanced state of consciousness that connects our thoughts, physical actions, and emotions in order to reach our inner selves, harmony, and happiness. Meditation leads to an understanding of the secret

Figure 24. Gin Zuo: Internal Contemplation

of life and death through advanced internal contemplation and a loss of all fear: She who does not know fear no longer has to pretend to be someone else. She is genuine, secure in herself, strong—and thus beautiful.

Since ancient times there have been innumerable avenues to attaining inner peace. One of the most effective has been the method presented here. The following requirements are necessary to enter into meditation with the proper spiritual and physical posture:

- Choose a clean and quiet place where you feel especially comfortable.

- Wash your hands and your face (this is of symbolic significance: Cleanse yourself).

- Wear comfortable, nonsynthetic clothing and take off your shoes.

- Sit on a comfortable cushion on which you can stay for extended periods of time. It is not necessary to sit in the lotus position; it is enough to cross your legs.

- Slightly bow your head and close your eyes.

- Relax your shoulders.

- Form your hands into bowls and place them a little below your navel. Place them on top of one another, yet not touching.

- Breathe only through your nose.

- Breathe out everything bad (thoughts, emotions, energies) in one fell swoop.

- Now slowly inhale everything good.

- Keep breathing in and out. Try to breathe slowly and silently.

- Your breathing will become natural and united with you.

- Try to stop thinking. While this is always the most difficult part, it is worth the effort. The goal of the exercise is to become "empty." If you concentrate only on your breathing, it will be easier to separate yourself from your thoughts.

If this is impossible for you, try using the following aid: Choose one word with a positive content (*sunlight* or *happiness* or the like) and say it over and over in your thoughts or out loud. You can also choose one of the following Buddhist meditation texts:

- Nan Mu—"largesse" (figure 25)

- Nan Mu Mo Ho Pan Lo Po Luo Mi—"great wisdom to reach the other side"* (figure 26)

- An Wu Loen Ni Sa Po Ho—"heart that cannot be broken" (figure 27)

- An Sho Do Li Sho Do Li Sho Mo Li Sho Mo Li Sa Po Ho—"body without pain, without fault, without need, without want" (figure 28)

- An Sho Li Sho Li Mo Ho Sho Li—"words without malice, without harm, without ignorance" (figure 29)

- An Fu Ze Luo Do No Ho Hu—"thoughts without hate, without fear" (figure 30)

---

* "The other side" in Buddhism means the world that Buddha saw during his "awakening"—a world without suffering.

Figure 25. Nan Mu: Largesse

Figure 26. Nan Mu Mo Ho Pan Lo Po Luo Mi:
Great Wisdom to Reach the Other Side

Figure 27. An Wu Loen Ni Sa Po Ho:
Heart that Cannot Be Broken

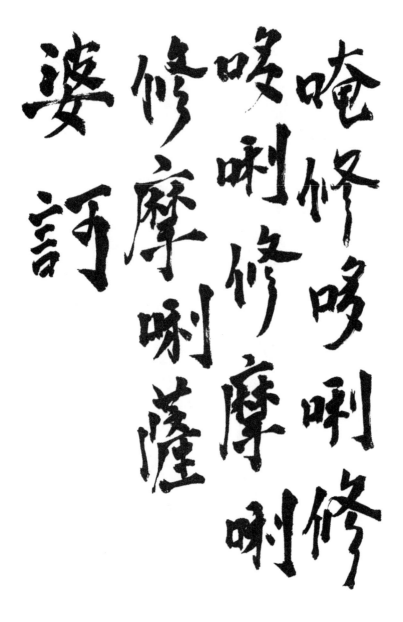

Figure 28. An Sho Do Li So Do Li Sho Mo Li Sho Mo Li Sa Po Ho:
Body without Pain, without Fault, without Need, without Want

Figure 29. An Sho Li Sho Li Mo Ho Sho Li:
Words without Malice, without Harm, without Ignorance

Figure 30. An Fu Ze Luo Do No Ho Hu:
Thoughts without Hate, without Fear

Repeat these phrases over and over again, until the first and the last words merge to become one. The rhythm will lead you to a melody that will facilitate internalizing the text. You are now learning to forget your emotions, your consciousness, and your thoughts.

Concentrate on the texts in a way that connects your breathing to the words, until neither is separate any longer. In this state your surroundings should no longer be perceptible to you.

This is only the beginning of meditation. In a sense you are still standing in the entrance hall and have to cross through several rooms in order to reach the holiest one.

To make your way to the inner area of the meditation temple, it is necessary to meditate on a regular basis (in the beginning for ten minutes every day). With increasing experience you should expand your meditation times (up to an hour a day). This will also improve your ability to block out thoughts and to become "empty."

During internal contemplation it is possible that you will experience internal pictures, such as a golden or white light, or a world more positive than you ever before perceived. These are "good" pictures. However, there are also "bad" pictures, for example ghosts and demons, that rise from your subconscious. Moreover, objects from your everyday life might also appear before your eyes, like a broom, a lamp, or a shopping cart. All these pictures arise from the depths of your soul and come up suddenly since you, during internal contemplation, are no longer able to suppress them.

What to do? You want to empty yourself, yet new pictures keep appearing. Since there is an infinite number of pictures, the only answer is to stop the influx (otherwise it is even possible to get entirely absorbed by them). The only way to do this is by continuing to repeat the meditation texts out loud. Don't get discouraged or focus on trying to rid your mind of thoughts; just relax and continue trying to focus on the texts.

In the next room of the meditation hall you are introduced to the chi. According to Chinese beliefs it is the strength of life, the source of all being. It is everywhere but is invisible; it is infinitely effective, but not affected itself. It is what one could call the "breath of life." In Buddhism, chi is the most natural thing. We encounter it wherever we look, inside and out.

For us it is important to connect meditation to chi. This can be accomplished in the following manner.

Take up your meditation position. Concentrate on your chi point, also called the "third eye": You find it where your nose and eyebrows intersect (diagram A).

Now concentrate on your head chakra—chakras are gates of energy that can be found on points all over the body, from head to toe; chi runs through them and fills us with the strength of life (diagram B).

Concentrate on your throat chakra, then on your hips, then the coccyx, and finally the sexual chakra. The sexual chakra is where sexual energy waits to be awakened.

Finally, concentrate on the navel chakra, then on the heart chakra, and then back on your chi point (diagram C).

Bring the chi from chakra to chakra. Remain with each until you can feel the chi (it usually resembles a warm sensation). Decide for yourself when to move on to the next chakra. The goal is to open all the energy points, in part to attain the beauty results that are no longer merely external, but of an internal nature as well. Through meditation you have become a different person and have made your interior more beautiful.

Imagination
HOW TO USE THE POWER OF IMAGINATION

The ability to imagine is often stronger than we think. All peoples, all cultures, all humans use the art of imagination whenever they want to obtain something that is present, yet still distant. In daily life this usually occurs at a subconscious level. In all spiritual traditions, there are ways to induce changes solely through the power of thoughts. Unfortunately, this power can also be used in negative ways—although this will always reflect back upon the person who does so. To enhance beauty, it is necessary to find out which techniques have positive effects on the internal organs so as to prompt

Figure 31. Fo: Buddhism

noticeable changes for the external body. "Beauty defects" can often be removed through imagination. However, this requires patient practicing of intense focusing.

How can you turn your beauty dream into reality? Of course you have to practice being disciplined—you can't imagine slender hips while at the same time eating everything fatty and sweet. Moreover, you need to carry out the physical and meditative exercises that have been described here.

Here's an example: You feel your breasts are too small and would be considerably more beautiful if they were only an inch bigger in circumference. To attain this goal without silicone, you should use the following exercise:

- Begin and end each day by imagining the breasts of your dreams for five minutes.

- During this fantasy, silently repeat, "grow, grow, grow . . ." Scientific studies have shown that this method does lead to results—despite widespread skepticism. It is probably because the soul is able to issue commands to the body. It is likely that illnesses can be influenced in the same way.

- Additionally, it is helpful to engage in physical exercises to attain the desired results. In this example, the third exercise in the section on breasts is recommended (pages 20–21).

- Practice the art of transmitting thoughts. Try to influence your environment in ways that will make people perceive you in ways you'd like. But don't overdo it, since the effects could be reversed!

Figure 32. Shian Shien Li: The Strength of the Imagination

Visualization

THE STRENGTH OF INTERNAL IMAGES

What you learned in the preceding chapter was the basis for what you can specifically do to positively influence your appearance from your internal side. We like to call this art "visualizing," since you no longer merely imagine the desired result. Rather, you are able to choose from the plethora of internal visions those that you desire. In other words: Visualizing is refined imagination, since you no longer have a headful of varied images but instead a concentrated focus. The breasts will once again serve as an example.

You imagine your dream breasts. Yet how can you be sure that this image is what you really want and not just an amalgam of all the pictures of breasts that you have seen so far?

This is how you can be sure: You will find what you consider to be right when you can bring it into harmony with everything else. The objective is not merely for you to have breasts as large or small as you desire them, but rather to reach an overall harmony in everything. Beauty is not perfection, but proportion.

Thus, when you visualize a part of your body, whichever one you want, you have to keep in mind that your body might prefer to remain the way it is. You must find out what it is that your body wants! And keep in mind: The world is beautiful because of its diversity, not because of its perfection. Diversity enables life, while perfection eliminates goals.

Figure 33. Du Lian: The Right Amount

Habits

HOW A RAINDROP BECOMES A RIVER

Lao-tzu says: "The softest will triumph over the hardest, the nonsubstance will penetrate the impenetrable hardness." What this Chinese wise man is describing is nothing more than water, the strength of which is also reflected in a German saying: "The steady drop will shape the rock." This natural law can be applied to our life without modifications: It is our good and bad habits that influence our personality, our health, our beauty, and our success. Unfortunately, we only rarely realize how bad habits over time start to take control of us. Here are some widespread examples:

- the cigarette after getting up

- starting work without breakfast

- candy as snacks

- cold meals

- sugared drinks (especially in the summer)

- a mixture of sweet and salty, warm and cold

- alcohol as a way to relax

- eating too fast

- watching TV while eating

Figure 34. Di Shui Zwan She: Steady Drips Shape the Stone

But these can be replaced by *good* habits. There are exercises that—when done daily, weekly, monthly, or yearly—are capable of creating an internally and externally beautiful person.

Exercises (Do Once a Day)

- Meditate for five minutes.

- Read at least one chapter in a book.

- Do a good deed.

- Compliment someone (even an animal).

- Walk for thirty minutes.

- Tidy up your home.

- Reflect on what you have done.

Exercises (Do Once a Week)

- Get out into nature.

- Clean your home.

- Go to bed early.

- Reflect on what you have done.

Exercises (Do Once a Month)

- Fast (see page 96).

- Go to the country.

- Buy one less thing.

- Forgo using the car.

- Donate something.

- Visit your parents.

- Meditate for a long time.

- Attend a cultural event.

- Do something special for (your) children.

- Give a gift to the one you love most.

- Give a gift to the one you like the least.

- Reflect on what you have done.

The calligraphy of figure 34 says that it is beneficial to internalize one's good habits to the point where they become second nature. This serves as a preventive measure against the most widespread disease of civilization, which is a decisive factor in hurting our health and thus our beauty: stress. Here are four exercises designed to alleviate stress.

1. Exercise (Do before Going to Sleep)

Every day, before going to bed, take a hot five-minute footbath. This will help you fall asleep faster, without lying awake for hours, thinking about problems.

2. Exercise (Do Anytime)

When you feel especially drained, press the first three fingers of both hands on the acupressure points of your ears, indicated in the diagram.

Proceed as follows: First press against points A, B, and C until they are hot. Then massage these points in the A, B, C order for nine seconds each. Now "fold" your ears: bend A down, C up, and B in. Press your palms against your ears and turn your hands nine times to the front and nine times to the back. Finally, massage the points in the order C, E, B, D, A.

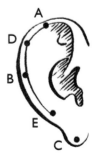

3. Exercise (Do Anytime)

Using the thumb and index finger of your right hand, massage the soft spot between the thumb and index finger on your left hand four times. From there, work your way up to the tip of the thumb (altogether for thirty-six seconds). Repeat this exercise with your left hand.

Using your thumb and index finger, press against the spot behind the joint of the pinkie four times. From there, work your way up to its tip (altogether for thirty-six seconds). Repeat this exercise with your other hand.

Now rub your hands until they are hot, fold them, and open them again right away. Repeat this three times.

4. Exercise (Do Anytime)

Rub your two middle fingers from the tip of your nose up to your hairline. Remain there with your fingers, spread your thumbs, and press these under your eyebrows and up to your temples. Rub your hands until they are hot and use them to cover your eyes for thirty-six seconds.

As you allow the tiny water droplets of your habits to increasingly converge into a river of daily routine, you will notice how your new internal beauty takes on a life of its own and starts to become noticeable on the outside as well.

Figure 35. Shi Guan Chong Tse Zian:
From Habit to Second Nature

Figure 36. Nei Tsai Mei: Internal Beauty

The Harmony of Internal and External Beauty

*E*veryone wants to be beautiful. What one person considers beautiful may appear ugly to another. We all have different tastes, and nature has room for people of all shapes, sizes, and colors. Apparently, nature is determined not to set limits for itself by any objective measures.

We have discovered that beauty is more than just outer appearances. It remains to be shown how it is possible to maintain internal as well as external beauty. The basis for this is the Taoist yin-yang teaching. Yin stands for the female and all that is associated with femininity; yang is the symbol for maleness. For health and beauty to reign, yin and yang must always be balanced and in harmony with one another.

Nothing represents this harmony better than the ancient yin-yang symbol: It connects the external and the internal in such a way that they form an infinite unity—which is what we aspire to.

Figure 37. Yin and Yang

Deep Cleaning
EVERYTHING GROWS FROM NOTHING

Everyone knows that daily cleansing is necessary for beauty and health. Here, however, we are not concerned with brushing the teeth or washing the face, but rather the cleansing of the internal organs.

The first chapter in the oldest Chinese medical book says, "He who wants to live long has to keep his intestines clean." The daily cleansing of the intestines is of highest importance among the Indian yogis as well. It is essential for clean skin, a pleasant odor, and stable health. This is because the daily cleansing fights the gases that form in the intestines during the night. Therefore, before going to bed it is advisable to use the toilet to excrete as much of the intestinal contents as possible. In this way you will be able to release many toxins and roughage. However, since there are still toxins at the end of the intestine, it should be cleaned with water. This is also necessary since present-day toilets, while very hygienic, are not constructed anatomically, meaning that the intestines are pressed together so tightly that it is impossible to empty them out completely. In contrast, ancient toilets were designed so that one had to kneel down to use them. This kept the spine straight; also, the intestines were relaxed and could be emptied easily. Today, rinsing the anus can help us attain the same results: It is able to remove or alleviate many problems, like bad breath, posture problems caused by gases, stomach ailments, digestion problems, skin blemishes, and sleep disorders.

To better visualize this concept, consider the following analogy: Imagine that you emptied your trash every day but never did so completely, instead leaving behind a bit. You are doing this day after day, week after week. Can you imagine what is happening in your garbage can? The tiny remnants can create huge problems.

The following exercise helps you to completely empty your garbage can.

Exercise

- While using the bathroom, concentrate only on what you are doing. Do not read or distract yourself otherwise. If you want to, close your eyes.

- Once you are done using the toilet, do not use toilet paper but rather go to the shower. Bend your knees, spread your legs, and direct the water on the anus. Try to relax your muscles and to let in a strong water stream. Rhythmically contract and relax your muscles. Do this for about three minutes so that the intestine can absorb the water.

- Leave the shower and get dressed.

- After about five to thirty minutes, you will feel a bubbling in your intestine. You will have the feeling of needing to use the bathroom. Do so and excrete the remainder of your intestinal content along with the water.

- Again use the shower (instead of toilet paper) to briefly cleanse the anus.

Most people would consider this a strange, cumbersome, and impractical exercise. Since it does take some time, it is best to do this exercise at night.

In addition to the daily cleansing of your intestines, you can significantly improve your skin and complexion in general by fasting one day a month—for hygienic reasons. The following procedure is recommended.

- Start reducing the size of your meals two days ahead of your fast. Do not eat anything fatty or fried. Don't smoke.

- Twelve hours before beginning your fast, consume only light or liquid foods for dinner (for example, rice, noodle, or vegetable soup).

- Start fasting at seven o'clock in the morning by drinking a glass of lukewarm water. Don't drink the water in big gulps, but rather "chew" on it. Repeat this at noon, and at seven at night.

- The following morning have oatmeal or rice milk for breakfast.

- Have only liquid foods for this day and the next.

- After the second day you can go back to your usual diet.

To suppress sudden feelings of hunger, you should follow these breathing techniques.

Exercise

Bring your tongue to the inside of your upper teeth and breathe over your tongue. Start by inhaling and holding your breath for nine seconds. Continue by exhaling for nine seconds through your nose. Again hold your breath for nine seconds. Continue breathing this way until the hunger disappears.

Figure 38. Chin: Purity

Figure 39. Ching: Clarity

While the cleansing of your intestines and the fasting will increase bodily hygiene, the "right" morning shower can also help this process. The following bathing process strengthens the body's immune system.

- The bathroom should be warm.

- Take as hot a shower as possible.

- Work the water from the bottom upward.

- Linger over each body part. The skin should be slightly red.

- Again work the water from the bottom upward, this time with cold water.

- Dry off with a rough towel.

Those who suffer from heart ailments or high blood pressure should not engage in this exercise.

The Proper Diet
EATING ACCORDING TO THE FIVE ELEMENTS TEACHING

The teaching of the five elements relies on the balance of the yin and yang polarities. The five elements make up the entire world: wood, fire, earth, metal, and water. The elements are related in the following way:

Wood brings about *fire;*
Fire brings about *ash;*
Ash turns into *earth;*

Earth gives *metal;*
Where there is *metal,* there is *water;*
Water allows *wood* to grow.

In Feng Shui teaching this relationship is called the "productive sequence." Its opposite is the "destructive sequence":

Wood fights against *earth;*
Earth fights against *water;*
Water fights against *fire;*
Fire fights against *metal;*
Metal fights against *wood.*

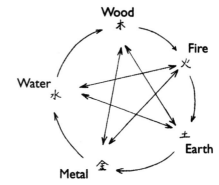

The organs of the body are also influenced by the five elements. They are related as follows:

ELEMENT	ORGANS	SENSORY ORGANS	OTHER BODY PARTS
Wood	Liver, gallbladder	Eyes	Tendons
Fire	Heart, small intestine	Tongue, mouth	Blood
Earth	Spleen, stomach	Skin	Muscles
Metal	Lungs, large intestine	Nose	Skin, hair
Water	Kidneys, bladder	Ears	Bones

The colors and tastes are also marked by the five elements:

ELEMENT	TASTE	COLOR
Wood	Sour	Green
Fire	Bitter	Red
Earth	Sweet	Yellow
Metal	Sharp	White
Water	Salty	Black

It is necessary to find out which element one belongs to. The method to determine this differs for men and women.

For women: Subtract 4 from the last two digits of your year of birth. Divide the result by 9. Usually a number with decimals will be the result. Only the first digit after the decimal point is significant for this inquiry. If the result is a natural number, use a zero as the digit after the decimal point. For example:

68 – 4 = 64 ÷ 9 = 7.1 (rounded); the 1 is your number

For men: Subtract the last two digits of your year of birth from the number 100 and divide the result by 9. If the result is a fraction, only the first digit after the decimal point is of importance. As for women, if the result is a natural number, use a zero as the digit after the decimal point. For example:

100 – 74 = 26 ÷ 9 = 2.8 (rounded); the 8 is your number

The relationship between elements and numbers is as follows:

Wood	1	2
Fire	3	4
Earth	5	6
Metal	7	8
Water	9	0

When assigning foods to elements you should not be surprised to see that some appear more than once. That is because the characterizations are based both on color and on taste.

Wood

Green beans, celery, parsley, zucchini, peas, broccoli, Chinese cabbage, spinach, peppermint, tomatoes, green apples, lemons, grapefruits, oranges, kiwi, peaches, cherries, pineapples, green olives, vinegar.

Fire

Carrots, red beans, eggplant, radishes, tomatoes, red apples, cherries, litchis, grapes, lamb, game, chili, green and black olives, green and black tea.

Earth

White, green, red, and black beans, pumpkin, yellow peppers, potatoes, corn, wheat, chestnuts, melons, yellow apples, papaya, mangos, pears, cherries, grapes, litchis, bananas, pineapples, tofu, sugar, honey, sesame, poultry, rabbit, fish, beef, eggs.

Metal

Radishes, onions, garlic, mushrooms, white morels, potatoes, ginger, pepper, pepperoni, rice, poultry, fish.

Water

Black beans, black sesame, black morels, black olives, seaweed, seafood, salt.

You now know your number and thus your element. You know which foods belong to which elements and have been introduced to the relationship of the five elements necessary for a yin and yang balance. What should your diet look like now? You can find out for yourself with the following example.

Your number is 1, thus you are wood. Water and fire are "friends" of wood. Thus, the proper diet for you consists of water and fire foods. "Enemies" of wood are metal and earth. Too much of these foods will be bad for you.

Proper Breathing
IN HARMONY WITH THE UNIVERSAL RHYTHM

You have probably noticed not only that in many exercises movement and concentration are important, but that breathing plays an important role, too. An analogy can clarify why this is true: If you are going on a hike and are consistently breathing incorrectly, you will quickly be out of breath. However, if you breathe properly, you can hike for several hours. The reason for this is the body's need to absorb oxygen, without which it can't function. Sports that take place outdoors in the fresh air are thus much healthier than those done inside.

When this book refers to "breathing," we usually refer to a very conscious exhaling and inhaling that is in harmony with your other movements, creating one rhythm. To breathe properly, follow these hints:

- Only breathe through your nose.

- Exhale in such a manner that you can feel your stomach contracting.

- Inhale in such a way that you feel as though the air will reach the diaphragm.

- Never breathe flatly, but always as deeply, long, and calmly as possible.

- If you do this for long enough, it will become second nature to you. You will no longer have to think about breathing properly—it will happen by itself.

- Once you accomplish this you will inhale chi, the universal life energy, with each breath you take.

Figure 40. Yang Xen Ze Tao: The Way to Health

Figure 41. Yuen: Unity

Chi Training
DAILY INTERACTIONS WITH THE ENERGY OF LIFE

As has been mentioned, chi is the mysterious strength that we—for lack of a better understanding—can only describe vaguely as "life energy." The ancient Japanese termed this phenomenon *ki,* the Indians *prana,* the Polynesians *mana,* the Greeks *pneuma,* and the Germanic peoples *odem.* Even though we can neither see nor touch this mysterious chi, even though we can neither create nor destroy it, we are still able to perceive it, to feel it inside, and even to train it to support our beauty efforts.

Exercise

- Find an airy and comfortable place.

- Wear clothing made of natural fibers.

- Sit down in the lotus position or with your legs crossed.

- Keep your spine straight.

- Make your hands into small bowls and place them on your knees.

- Breathe slowly through your nose.

- Close your eyes and focus on the chi point (the "third eye")

- Let go of all thoughts.

- Lightly clatter your teeth thirty times. Cross the index and middle fingers of each hand while doing this and place your palms against your ears. While you are clattering your teeth, tap your occipital bone with your fingers.

- Again place your hands on your knees. While keeping your mouth closed, make a counterclockwise circle with your tongue thirty-six times, and then a clockwise circle thirty-six times.

- Rinse your mouth thirty-six times with the saliva produced during the exercise.

- Swallow the saliva in three swallows.

- Now concentrate on your breast chakra.

- Briefly hold your breath and rub your hands until they are hot.

- Massage your loins thirty-six times; do not breathe while doing this.

- Exhale and inhale deeply.

- Concentrate on your navel chakra until you can feel this region begin to get warmer.

- With your arms extended, draw a small circle in the air thirty-six times.

- Extend your legs forward.

- Cross your fingers just above your head and draw a semicircle to your thighs with your arms three times in a row.

- Return to your initial sitting position.

- Repeat the saliva rinsing three times.

- Now you should be able to feel the chi inside you.

Figure 42. Chi: Strength of Life

Exercise

- Lie flat on your back.

- Spread your legs wide, your palms touching the ground.

- Inhale deeply through your nose and hold your breath for as long as possible.

- Exhale silently through your mouth.

The secret of this exercise lies in extending the time you hold your breath every day. Taoist priests can count up to one thousand while holding their breath—but this takes years of practice.

Exercise

The following exercise is not only for increased beauty, but also for strengthening of your sexual prowess.

- Lie down flat on your back.

- Spread your legs slightly, your palms touching the ground.

- Contract your anus.

- Place both your hands on the lower part of your stomach and inhale deeply through your nose. Exhale silently through your mouth while relaxing your anus. Place your hands back on the ground.

- Repeat this exercise eight times. Hold your breath the last time, for as long as you can. Press your middle finger thirty times against the root chakra. Exhale silently through your mouth.

- Rub your hands until they are hot and massage your thighs thirty times on the inside and the outside.

- Again rub your hands until they are hot, then rest your face in them. While doing this, clatter with your teeth thirty-six times.

- Again rub your hands until they are hot. Cross the index and middle fingers of each hand and place your palms against your ears. Tap the occipital bone thirty times with your fingers.

- Again rub your hands until they are hot. Massage your breasts thirty-six times.

- Rub your hands until they are hot and move them from your breasts to your navel thirty-six times.

- Rub your hands until they are hot, place the left hand on the navel, turn to your side, and massage your groin thirty-six times using your right hand.

- With the middle finger of your left hand, press down on the coccyx thirty-six times.

- Rub your hands until they are hot and place your right hand on your navel. Turn to your side and massage your groin thirty-six times using your left hand.

- With the middle finger of your right hand, press down on the coccyx thirty-six times.

- Slowly rub your lower stomach with your left hand 120 times.

- Repeat this with your right hand.

- For men: Massage your testicles 120 times with your left hand. Repeat this with your right hand.

- For women: massage your right breast with your left hand 120 times and your left breast with your right hand 120 times.

- Lie down flat and relax.

Even though this exercise may seem complicated, it is good to do it on a regular basis. Not only do you learn to discover your chi, but you develop it as well. That this is a good skill to have was stated by Men-tse twenty-three hundred years ago: "He who develops his chi will find the right path."

氣乃至大至剛至氣所不在

Figure 43. Chi Nei Da Ze Gau Wu Suo Bu Zai:
Chi Is the Strongest and Greatest There Is, It Is Everywhere

Appendix

The Four-Week Beauty Program

In this section beauty is enhanced through the combined elements of meditation, acupressure, and nutrition. If you can, do this program while on vacation so that you can truly benefit from the relaxation it engenders.

Start by reading this section in its entirety to get a good overview of what the program entails.

CHI MEDITATION

1. Search for your "third eye." You will find it by visualizing a straight line from your nose to your hairline. At the same time, visualize another line connecting the highest points of your eyebrows. Your third eye is where these two lines intersect.
2. Visualize this point as a third eye and concentrate on it with every breath you take.
3. For fifteen minutes in the morning and fifteen minutes in the afternoon, change your regular breathing rhythm: Instead of the normal inhaling and exhaling, exhale twice for every one breath you take.

4. Choose a word to repeat over and over while practicing your new breathing technique. This word should relate to beauty, such as *shine, light,* or *sun.* The word should become *your* word; you will use it from now on to orient yourself.

5. Listen to yourself while you breathe. Try to do your one breath inhaling, two breaths exhaling as slowly as possible. This is easiest when you don't think about it.

6. For five minutes in the morning and five minutes in the afternoon, lie down and cup your hands at the level of your pelvis as though you were holding water in them.

7. Exercise 7 is a variation of exercise 6. Place your cupped hands above the concentration point on your forehead and hold them there for five minutes. Your hands should not touch your forehead.

WEEK ONE		WEEK TWO	
Monday	Meditation 1	Monday	Meditation 1–7 Exercise 1
Tuesday	Meditation 1, 2	Tuesday	Meditation 1–7 Exercise 1
Wednesday	Meditation 1–3	Wednesday	Meditation 1–7 Exercise 1, 2
Thursday	Meditation 1–4	Thursday	Meditation 1–7 Exercise 1, 2
Friday	Meditation 1–5	Friday	Meditation 1–7 Exercise 1–3
Saturday	Meditation 1–6	Saturday	Meditation 1–7 Exercise 1–3
Sunday	Meditation 1–7	Sunday	Meditation 1–7 Exercise 1–3

WEEK THREE		WEEK FOUR	
Monday	Meditation 1–7 Exercise 1–4	Monday	Meditation 1–7 Exercise 1–7 Menu 1, 5, 7
Tuesday	Meditation 1–7 Exercise 1–4	Tuesday	Meditation 1–7 Exercise 1–7 Menu 2, 6, 9
Wednesday	Meditation 1–7 Exercise 1–5	Wednesday	Meditation 1–7 Exercise 1–8 Menu 3, 4, 8
Thursday	Meditation 1–7 Exercise 1–5	Thursday	Meditation 1–7 Exercise 1–8 Menu 2, 5, 9
Friday	Meditation 1–7 Exercise 1–6	Friday	Meditation 1–7 Exercise 1–9 Menu 3, 6, 8
Saturday	Meditation 1–7 Exercise 1–6	Saturday	Meditation 1–7 Exercise 1–9 Menu 1, 4, 7
Sunday	Meditation 1–7 Exercise 1–6	Sunday	Meditation 1–7 Exercise 1–9 Menu 2, 6, 9

CHI ACUPRESSURE EXERCISES

1. Exercise

Locate your chi point and concentrate on it while keeping your eyes closed. You'll know you have found it when the point feels like it is shining brightly inside you (diagram A).

A

2. Exercise

B

Take a deep breath. While exhaling, tap the area between your nose and chin and around the mouth, using your fingertips. The tapping of your fingers should resemble the staccato of playing the piano (diagram B). Repeat this exercise four times in a row.

3. Exercise

Place both thumbs on the chi points behind your earlobes (where you would normally apply perfume). Move both your hands toward your chin, moving neither too quickly nor too slowly. Close your eyes while doing this and open them only after the ninth movement (diagram C). Do this four times in every session.

C

4. Exercise

Start by washing your face around your nose. Collect lukewarm water in your hands and pull it into your nose by inhaling forcefully. Release the water by exhaling powerfully (diagram D). Do this nine times.

D

5. Exercise

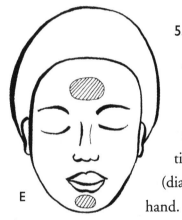

E

Apply water to your face. Yet instead of massaging it into the skin with circular movements, tap it into your skin using the fingers of one hand—nine times at your forehead and chin areas (diagram E). Repeat this using your other hand.

6. Exercise

Now apply water to your face by tapping it onto your cheeks (diagram F). Repeat this process using your other hand.

F

7. Exercise

Apply your facial moisturizer as follows: Using the fingertips of your right hand, rub the cream from your right temple in eight circular movements to the left temple, as shown in diagram G. The ninth movement leads along the cheekbone to the chin. Carry out the same movements in the opposite direction with your left hand.

G

H

8. Exercise

Treat the area above your lips by applying the cream with your right hand. Begin at the right corner of your mouth and move to the left corner and back using circular motions (diagram H). Do the reverse with your left hand.

9. Exercise

Rest your fingertips against your nose and spread the facial or eye creme in nine soft circular motions around your eyes (diagram I).

I

Figure 44. Shen: Beauty of the Spirit

Figure 45. Gin: Silence

Figure 46. Li: Power

CHI MENU

Appetizers (For Two People)

I. CHICKEN WITH BEAN SPROUTS

$^1/_2$ pound chicken breast, sliced thin

I garlic clove, crushed

I pound soybean sprouts

I tablespoon canola or safflower oil

soy sauce or salt and pepper to taste

In a saucepan over moderate heat, sauté the garlic and chicken in the oil. When the meat becomes white, add the soybean sprouts. Add seasoning and serve immediately.

2. CHICKEN AND GREEN BEAN STIR-FRY

3 dried chili peppers, minced

2 garlic cloves, minced

2 teaspoons grated fresh ginger root

I tablespoon canola or safflower oil

$^1/_2$ pound chicken breast, sliced thin

I pound green beans

2 tablespoons soy sauce

2 teaspoons sugar

2 teaspoons sesame oil

In a saucepan over moderate heat, briefly sauté chilis, garlic, and ginger in the oil. Add the chicken and sauté until it is white. Add the beans, cover, and let steam until the beans are crisp-tender. Add soy sauce, sugar, and sesame oil. Serve hot.

3. CUCUMBER SALAD

I cucumber

I dried chili pepper, minced

I garlic clove, minced

1 tablespoon soy sauce

1 tablespoon sesame oil

1 teaspoon sugar

After peeling the cucumber, cut it lengthwise into thin slices. Mix the remaining ingredients with the cucumber and serve.

Main Courses (For Two People)

4. MISO CHICKEN NOODLE SOUP

2 or 3 cloves garlic, minced

1 tablespoon fresh ginger root, peeled and minced

2 medium carrots, sliced thin

2 stalks celery, sliced thin

2 tablespoons canola or safflower oil

2 teaspoons dark sesame oil

6 cups water or chicken or vegetable stock

$1/2$ pound chicken breast cut into bite-size pieces

$1/4$ pound udon rice noodles (or substitute spaghetti)

$1/4$ pound snow peas, sliced on the diagonal

1 sweet red pepper, sliced thin

2 cups fresh spinach or other greens, coarsely chopped

$1/4$ cup parsley, minced

$1/2$ cup scallions, chopped fine

2 tablespoons miso (a fermented soybean paste)*

soy sauce and black pepper to taste

In a soup kettle sauté the garlic and ginger briefly in 1 tablespoon canola or safflower oil and 1 teaspoon sesame oil. Add the carrots and celery and sauté for another 2 or 3 minutes. Cover with water or stock and simmer until vegetables are almost tender.

---

*Miso is available at oriental specialty food stores or natural food stores. It is Japanese rather than Chinese, but appropriate here because it stimulates good digestion. Brown rice miso or sweet white miso are particularly good in this soup.

In a separate pan, sauté the chicken in remaining oil until white and set aside.

Add noodles to the simmering soup. When they are almost done, add the red pepper, peas, greens, and chicken (with its cooking juices). When the vegetables are just tender, add parsley and scallions and simmer for one more minute. Remove from heat. Thin the miso paste with a few tablespoons of the soup broth, then add it to the soup. Season with soy sauce or salt and pepper to taste, and serve hot.

5. SOYBEAN AND RICE SOUP

1 15-oz. can soybeans, drained

$^1/_3$ pound rice

$^1/_2$ pound zucchini, very finely chopped

2 stalks celery, finely chopped

1 garlic clove, finely chopped

sesame oil

salt and pepper

dried basil

Place the first five ingredients in a pot and cover with water to twice their depth. Add a few drops of oil, some pepper, salt, and dried basil. Let cook for thirty minutes. Serve the soup hot.

6. ORIENTAL NOODLES WITH CHICKEN

$^2/_3$ pound spaghetti, or Chinese or Japanese noodles

$^1/_2$ onion, finely chopped

1 tablespoon canola or safflower oil

$^1/_2$ pound chicken breast, cut in slices

salt and pepper

1 tablespoon curry powder

$^3/_4$ pound soybean sprouts

sesame oil

Boil and drain the noodles. In a saucepan, sauté the onion and add the chicken breast, salt, pepper, and curry powder. Once the meat is done, add the soybean sprouts and stir-fry for thirty seconds. Add the cooked noodles and mix thoroughly. Finish by adding a few drops of sesame oil. Serve hot.

Desserts (For Two People)

7. TROPICAL FRUIT SALAD WITH ALMONDS

    1 mango
    1 papaya
    1 banana
    1 kiwi
    the juice of 1 lemon
    5 tablespoons honey
    1 ounce almonds, peeled and chopped

Peel and dice the fruits and mix with the lemon juice and honey. Sprinkle in the almonds. Serve chilled.

8. RED BEAN MOON CAKES

    4 cups unbleached white flour
    1 tablespoon baking powder
    1/2 teaspoon salt
    1/2 cup sugar
    1/2 cup unsalted butter, melted and cooled slightly, or 1/2
    cup vegetable oil
    3 large eggs
    6 to 7 tablespoons cold water
    1 egg beaten with 2 tablespoons water
    sweet red bean paste* filling

*Sweet red bean paste is available in Asian specialty markets.

Combine flour, baking powder, and salt.

In a separate large bowl, beat the eggs with the sugar for about ten minutes. Add the melted butter or oil, the water, and the dry ingredients and stir until a rough dough forms. Roll it into a long rope $1^1/_4$ inches thick, and cut into 24 pieces.

Preheat the oven to 375°.

Using your hands, press each dough section into a 3-inch circle with the edges pinched thinner than the center. Place a portion of the filling in the center, gather up the edges of the dough to meet in the center, and pinch to seal. Roll each piece of dough into a ball between your hands and flatten it to a 3-inch round cake.

Place the cakes one inch apart on an ungreased cookie sheet. Brush the tops with egg and water mixture and bake for 25 to 30 minutes until golden brown. Cool and serve. Makes 24 cakes.

9. MANGO CRÈME

I mango

I pint heavy cream

Peel the mango, remove the seed, and purée the fruit in a blender or food processor. In a separate bowl, whip the cream until stiff. Fold the mango purée into the cream. Serve in a cocktail glass, garnished with honey.

Figure 47. Chien: Health

Figure 48. Chie: Cleanliness

The Bathing, Beauty, and Health Program

Bathing is good for your health both inside and out. Because of its relaxing qualities, taking a bath can make you more beautiful. At this point, we would like to demonstrate how it is possible to combine chi-acupressure and bathing. These special preparations for baths enhance beauty, prevent aging, and are good for your health as well.*

The duration of a bath should be about ten to fifteen minutes. The temperature depends on individual preference. All applications are a combination of Taoist acupressure and traditional Chinese medicine.

1. For Dry Skin

Preparation: Place two tablespoons of almonds into a net and place them in the bathwater. Add two tablespoons of sesame oil and ten drops of lily oil.

Lie down in the tub, close your eyes, and concentrate on the heart chakra.

2. For Oily Skin

Preparation: Cut the peels of an orange and a lemon into small pieces and place them in a net along with one tablespoon of green tea. Place the net in the bathwater.

Lie down in the tub, close your eyes, and concentrate on the navel chakra.

---

* Some of the ingredients were introduced to China only in recent times, yet are nonetheless key components of the recipe.

3. For Rough Skin

Preparation: Add ten drops of lavender oil to the hot bathwater. Put two tablespoons of fennel seeds along with four minced cloves of garlic in a net and suspend it in the water.

Lie down in the tub, close your eyes, and concentrate on your sexual chakra.

4. For Impure Skin

Preparation: Place four tablespoons of pine needles, twenty dried willow leaves, half a chopped onion, and an orange peel in a net and suspend it in the water.

Lie down in the tub, close your eyes, and concentrate on the middle of the soles of your feet.

5. For Fever

Preparation: Add one tablespoon of olive oil to the water. Suspend a net with twenty chopped ginger slices in it.

Lie down in the tub, close your eyes, and concentrate on the acupressure points in your temples. While doing this, massage the spots between the thumb and index fingers of both hands for five minutes each.

6. For Constipation

Preparation: Put one tablespoon of black sesame seeds, one chopped onion, and one tablespoon of chopped almonds in a net. Suspend in the water.

Lie down in the tub, close your eyes, and concentrate on the navel chakra. While doing this, massage the outsides of your calves.

Figure 49. Chin Song: Relaxation

7. For Swollen Feet

Preparation: Place two tablespoons of red and two tablespoons of black soybeans in a net along with two tablespoons of wheat grains. Suspend the net in the bathwater.

Lie down in the tub, close your eyes, and concentrate on the acupressure point at the bottom of your collarbone.

8. For Headaches

Preparation: Place two tablespoons of green tea leaves, ten chopped ginger slices, and one chopped celery stick in a net. Suspend the net in the bath.

Lie down in the tub, close your eyes, and concentrate on the acupressure point at the hairline on the back of your neck. While doing this, massage the soles of your feet.

9. For Stress

Preparation: Add one tablespoon of sesame oil to the bathwater. Place two tablespoons of uncooked rice and one chopped, unpeeled, raw potato in a net. Suspend the net in the water.

Lie down in the tub, close your eyes, and concentrate on the end of the coccyx. While doing this, massage the soles of your feet.

10. For Digestion Problems

Preparation: Add ten drops of sandalwood oil to the bathwater. Place three tablespoons of soybeans, two tablespoons of fennel seeds, and one tablespoon of rice in a net and suspend it in the water.

Lie down in the tub, close your eyes, and massage the spots beneath your shoulder blades. Also massage the heels of your feet.

11. For Coughs

Preparation: Add twenty drops of orange oil and one tablespoon of honey to the bathwater. Place the chopped peel of a grapefruit and a sliced pear in a net. Suspend the net in the water.

Lie down in the tub, close your eyes, and concentrate on the middle of your neck and the top of your spinal cord.

12. For Muscle Aches

Preparation: Add one tablespoon of salt to the water. Put one tablespoon of pine needles, two tablespoons of black soybeans, and five chopped ginger slices in a net. Suspend the net in the water.

Lie down in the tub, close your eyes, and massage the underside of your upper arms as well as the front of your calves.

13. For Nervousness

Preparation: Place one tablespoon of rose petals, one tablespoon of wheat grains, and ten chopped dried plums in a net. Suspend the net in the water, then add ten drops of rose oil.

Lie down in the tub, close your eyes, and concentrate on the bottom of your collarbone. Massage your temples while doing this.

14. For a Lack of Appetite

Preparation: Place half a chopped carrot, five garlic cloves, one-half tablespoon of black pepper, and two tablespoons of black sesame in a net. Suspend it in the water.

Lie down in the tub, close your eyes, and massage the area between your shoulder blades and hipbones, as well as the soles of your feet.

15. For Rheumatism

Preparation: Add ten drops of Tiger Balm oil to the bathwater. Place four tablespoons of pine needles and half a sliced seeded papaya in a net. Suspend the net in the water.

Lie down in the tub, close your eyes, and concentrate on the throat chakra. While doing this, massage the acupressure points at the back of your knees.

16. For Flatulence

Preparation: Add ten drops of Tiger Balm oil to the bathwater. Place the chopped peel of a grapefruit, one tablespoon of green tea leaves, and one tablespoon of fennel seeds in a net. Suspend the net in the water.

Lie down in the tub, close your eyes, and concentrate on the bottom of your collarbone. Massage the lower part of your stomach.

17. For Bronchitis

Preparation: Add ten drops of Tiger Balm oil to the bathwater. Place ten dried medlar (loquat) leaves, one finely chopped pear, half a finely chopped grapefruit peel, and two tablespoons of chopped peanuts into a net. Suspend the net in the water.

Lie down in the tub, close your eyes, and concentrate on the head and navel chakras. Massage your shoulders.

18. For Acne

Preparation: Put one chopped celery stick, two tablespoons of green tea leaves, twenty dried willow leaves, ten dried plums, and ten raisins in a net. Suspend the net in the water.

Lie down in the tub, close your eyes, and massage the area between your chest and navel.

19. For the Flu

Preparation: Add ten drops of Tiger Balm oil and one tablespoon of honey to the bathwater. Put four chopped garlic cloves, ten thin carrot slices, and one chopped onion in a net. Suspend the net in the water.

Lie down in the tub, close your eyes, and massage your temples, your neck, and the top of your spinal cord.

20. For Eczema

Preparation: Add four tablespoons of white vinegar to the bathwater. Place four tablespoons of pine needles in a net and suspend it in the water.

Lie down in the tub, close your eyes, and concentrate on your ribs and your heart chakra. Massage your Achilles tendon.

Figure 50. Shui: Water

Figure 51. Yu: Elegance

From the Empress's Treasure Box

LITTLE TRICKS FOR LITTLE EMERGENCIES

These tips are designed for situations in which a quick fix is necessary. However, they can also be used in less urgent situations.

You Ate Too Much Garlic

There are several ways to deal with the unpleasant smell of garlic: You can drink one glass of milk or tea; you can chew gum or use a mouthwash. However, nothing is more effective than to eat a small bunch of parsley, which will also help your iron intake.

You Have the Hiccups

There are several ways to suppress hiccups: Drink half a glass of water in three gulps; after exhaling, hold your nose closed and hold your breath.

You can also use chopsticks to create a cross over your drinking glass and then drink out of each of the four "segments." While this may sound laughable, it works.

If you have this problem frequently, break up an eggshell, cook it for twenty minutes with three cups of water, strain, and drink the solution. This recipe also works for flatulence.

You Need to Wash Your Hair but Have No Time

Take a cotton ball, soak it in rubbing alcohol, and dab it against the roots of your hair. Massage your scalp for three minutes and brush your hair from the back forward.

You Have a Cold but Need to Attend a Meeting

Drink two glasses of cola that has been heated together with ten thick ginger slices. Add two tablespoons of honey and the juice of a lemon and drink the mixture. This recipe is very popular in Hong Kong.

You Have Athlete's Foot

The treatment and cure for this fungal disease usually takes a few weeks. But an ancient Chinese recipe helps—if the fungus is still in a relatively contained area—within three days.

Prepare the following footbath: one quart of water and one quart of vinegar. Heat the mixture until it is as hot as you can stand. Bathe your feet in it for ten to twenty minutes at least once a day.

You Have Dandruff

Place whole-wheat flour and water in a one-to-two ratio in a pot. Let simmer over low heat until the mixture thickens. Let the mixture cool off and then mix it with the whites of two eggs. Then wash your hair without shampoo and apply the mixture. Wrap your hair in a towel for five minutes, rinse the mixture out, and then dry your hair.

You Have a Headache

Press the thumb and index finger of your right hand against the soft spot between the thumb and index finger of your left hand, and vice versa. Press on this spot until you no longer feel any sensations in the area. Now, again using your thumb and index finger, press against your earlobes and move the corner of your ears upward, until you lose feeling.

Figure 52. Yun: Charm

You Are Stressed Out

Worries keep you up at night and you feel exhausted in the morning. With your index and middle fingers, press against your temples, while using your thumbs to press against the hairline on your neck. Work the thumbs from there to the other fingers, slowly moving along while exerting pressure. Always press firmly to lose feeling in the area being touched.

You Suddenly Have a Stomachache

Place your hands on your knees and spread out your fingers. Press your ring finger forcefully into your flesh until you lose feeling in the area.

You Feel Weak and Look Pale

Take a hot footbath and, using your top three fingers, massage your ears. Start by pressing against your earlobe from the top and continue by rolling over the edge until you no longer feel any pain.

Dry off your feet and tap your heels with the knuckles of your fist until you lose feeling.

You Are Constipated

Dissolve two tablespoons of salt in warm water and drink the solution.

You Want to Use False Eyelashes

Remove every second hair of the false eyelashes. This will make them look more natural.

Figure 53. Huo: Activity

Figure 54. Yen: Meaningfulness

You Want to Give Your Hair an Instant Silky Shine

Wet your hair with hot water, pour a shot glass of white vinegar over it, and massage in the vinegar. Follow by rinsing, washing, and drying.

You Want Your Skin to Be Smoother Right Away

Separate an egg white into two halves. Rub one half against your face and wash it off with lukewarm water. Now rub the second half on your face and let it dry for about five to ten minutes. Then wash it off with warm water and dry it carefully with a towel.

You Have Bad Breath

For this problem most Americans and Europeans reach for chewing gum. This unfortunately does not resolve the underlying problem, which is most often related to the teeth or to stomach bacteria. For emergencies (not for general healing), the Chinese use four leaves of green tea. Chew these leaves until they lose their taste.

You Have a Toothache

Massage the painful spot in your mouth with salt.

You Want to Prevent Aging Spots

Starting when you are fifty, drink the juice of one carrot every day.

Figure 55. Chin Tuen: Youth

Figure 56. Che Chou: Modesty

Figure 57. Chi Che: Personality

The Fifty-Point Program for Beauty and Eternal Youth

This books seeks to convey ancient Chinese knowledge regarding beauty and aging. In the Empire of the Middle Kingdom, people gain more value and respect as they age. This Eastern mind-set is very different from the Western viewpoint. The West is preoccupied with looking younger; signs of aging are reminders of death. In Asia, however, age brings greater beauty and wisdom; it is what we all look forward to.

However, if you still want to fight the aging process, you can look younger by following the fifty points outlined below.

1. Never stop learning.
2. Always stand on your own two feet.
3. Keep your distance from doubts.
4. Know that you are not the only one with desires.
5. Learn to understand others.
6. Follow your heart.
7. Strive to understand yourself.
8. Strive to understand humankind.
9. Practice being alone among people.
10. Practice being together with people.
11. Don't expect anything.
12. Don't be too happy about something.
13. Don't get too upset about something.
14. Trust your strength.
15. Never lose your capacity to be amazed.

16. Let patience be your steady companion.

17. Laud your critics.

18. Examine your outer appearance in the mirror—and your internal appearance by the responses of others.

19. Treat everything in life equally.

20. Help anyone anywhere.

21. Don't search for profit.

22. Be careful with your words.

23. Control your thoughts.

24. Be happy when somebody else is happy.

25. Be empathetic.

26. Don't be arrogant.

27. Broaden your time horizons.

28. Take care of those who are sad.

29. Stick first to love, then to people, then to the law.

30. Practice forgiving.

31. Don't compliment falsely.

32. Eliminate fear.

33. Live what you know.

34. Be aware of your responsibility.

35. Consider your accomplishments natural.

36. Fear your ability more than dangers.

37. See like the blind, hear like the deaf.

38. Don't consider success a steady companion.

39. Walk softly.

40. Enjoy work.

41. Be a helper to justice.

42. Learn to serve.

43. Consider the invisible visible.

44. Be good.

45. Be courageous.

46. Be respectful.

47. Be faithful.

48. Search for wisdom.

49. Unite beauty and attraction.

50. Don't be fooled by beauty.

"The noble promotes beauty in humans."

—**Confucius**

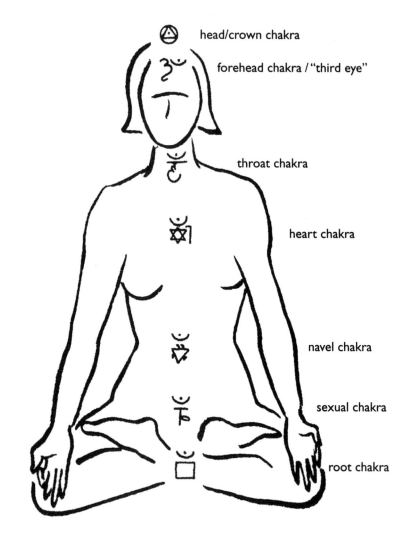

head/crown chakra

forehead chakra / "third eye"

throat chakra

heart chakra

navel chakra

sexual chakra

root chakra

Overview of the Chakras